BRACKLEY TEACHERS' CENTRE

GW01161773

A FIRST LOOK AT
COSTUME

by MARGARET CRUSH · Illustrations by FAITH JAQUES

FRANKLIN WATTS
London

Franklin Watts Limited,
26 Albemarle Street,
London, W.1.

SBN 85166 271 4
© 1972 Franklin Watts Limited
Reprinted 1974 and 1977.

Note
Especially for the Middle Ages period, there are many names for the same garment. This book has tried for consistency, but sometimes you may find in other books the same type of garment called a "supertunic", a "tunic", a "surcote", a "tabard", etc.

Photoset by BAS Printers Limited, Wallop, Hampshire
Printed in Great Britain by Sackville Press Billericay Ltd.

CONTENTS

About Costume	4
800's	6
1000's	7
1170's	8
1340's	9
1360's	10
1400's	11
Peasants in the Middle Ages, 800–1400	12
1450's	14
1480's	15
1500's	16
1540's	17
1570's	18
1600's	19
The Growth of the Middle Classes, 1400–1600	20
1620's	22
1640's	23
1650's	24
1660's	25
1690's	26
1720's	27
1740's	28
1770's	29
Country and Townsfolk, 1600–1770	30
1790's	32
1810's	33
1830's	34
1850's	35
1880's	36
1890's	37
1900's	38
1910's	39
The Working Classes, 1770–1910	40
1920's	42
1930's	43
1940's	44
1950's	45
Glossary/Index	46

ABOUT COSTUME

Costume is the word used to describe the changing styles (or **fashions**) of clothes in history. Over the years fashions have changed many times. Often, people got bored with the style they were wearing. Sometimes, changes in their way of life meant different kinds of clothes, e.g. factory women in World War II found trousers more sensible than skirts.

In the past styles changed fairly slowly, sometimes taking 50 or more years. People seldom saw new fashions, because **travel** was difficult and **printed books** were scarce. Nearer our own times, as both became common, fashion changes speeded up.

The pictures show clothes worn all over Europe and in European colonies, such as America and Australia, since about the time when the first European styles evolved from the **fitted** animal skins worn by barbarians in cold northern lands, and the **drapery** of the Greeks and Romans from warmer climates.

Over the years fashion was affected by **different countries** at different times. When Spain opened up the New World, other nations adopted her stiff and formal stomacher, ruff and farthingale. Trousers, previously worn only by boys, sailors and workmen, were adopted by young English gentlemen who approved of the rule of the workers started by the French Revolution.

The pictures show typical clothes of each period, mainly those worn by the people who were reasonably well off. The **labels** point out the important or interesting features of each period and more details are at the back and in the **Picture Glossary**.

Styles like this man's were probably worn on voyages to the New World by Leif Ericson and his men (compare the shape of the cap with the Viking helmet in the circle on page 7).

Obviously, not everyone wore exactly the styles shown, any more than we all wear the same things today. People have always worn clothes they themselves **like**. Also, **older** people tend to wear the styles of their youth, whereas **young** people enjoy being up to the minute. At every period the poorer people wore plainer, simpler clothes and some pages especially show these.

For centuries **men** were as brightly dressed as women. Then, about 1800 **women** dressed more gaily. Today, as the sexes more and more share the same way of life, their clothes are getting more **alike**, e.g. women wear trouser suits and men's clothes are brighter.

The pictures also show what **children** wore at each period. Children were often dressed uncomfortably as miniature adults. Often their clothes showed the way grown-up clothes would develop. Around 1570 boys started to wear the knee-length breeches which their fathers would not wear for another 20 years or so. Little girls of the 1790's wore the simple muslin dresses their mothers would wear 20 or 30 years later.

On each page, to help relate the clothes to the times when they were worn, a circle shows a famous **person** living at that time and a square shows a notable **event**.

It is fascinating to try to date old pictures by the clothes people are wearing in them. The fashions shown have been stopped at the 1950's, to let you try to work out which fashions since then will be selected by **costume historians** as typical of the times.

The basic two-piece costume of the 1890's as worn differently by a well-to-do lady and a working class woman.

Compare the boy's knee breeches with his father's trunk hose. The very young boy is not yet breeched—he still wears a long gown.

The Vikings

Charlemagne

For hundreds of years both before and after this date, men, women and children wore simple, plain clothes based on a sack-like woollen **tunic**. Over it, women and girls wore a **supertunic**, and they covered their hair with a long **veil**. Because homes were so cold, clothes were wrinkled up into cosy folds. Out of doors, everyone wore warm **cloaks**.

800's

Leif Ericson

The Crusades

Now men also were wearing supertunics. On their legs they wore loose, floppy **braies**, covered with **bandages**. Only noblemen could wear these bandages criss-crossed. Sometimes men wore a pointed **cap**, but usually went **bare-headed**. Girls could leave their hair unveiled. Babies were tightly **swaddled** (see p. 12), as Christ had been 1000 years before.

1000's

pointed cap
tunic
bandages
supertunic
braies
tunic
loose hair
cloak
tunic
socks
bandages
shorter veil
mantle
supertunic
tunic

Murder of Becket

St. Francis

Belts and **girdles** became very popular. The new slinky tunics of women and girls were called **kirtles**, and the **hanging sleeves** of their softly pleated supertunics almost reached the ground. Some girls covered their plaits with silk sheaths called **fouriaux**. Under their hats or hoods men wore little close fitting caps called **coifs**.

1170's

Chaucer

The Black Death

The Crusaders had brought back many gorgeous new Eastern materials. Men's stockings (**hose**) were often of different hues and the edges of their gay clothes were **dagged** into fancy patterns. The **hood** (worn today by friars) was popular. Women covered their hair with netted **frets** and borrowed the idea of the **surcote** (worn by Crusaders over armour).

1340's

hood
cotehardie
gipon
hose

chaplet
kirtle
sleeveless surcote

fillet
cloak with dagged edges
gipon

fillet
fret
barbette
surcote
kirtle

Hundred Years' War

The Black Prince

Men extended the pointed parts of their hoods (the **liripipe**) until they almost swept the ground. And they lengthened the feet of their hose too. The sides of the women's surcotes were cut right away to show off the kirtle underneath. Indeed, fashions became so outrageous and extravagant that in England special **laws** were passed to control dress.

1360's

- gipon
- hoods with long liripipes
- belt
- very pointed soled hose
- pocket
- chaplet
- kirtle
- fillet
- sideless surcote
- kirtle

Joan of Arc

Battle of Agincourt

Now the belt became a symbol of manhood. Boys did not wear belts and it was a terrible disgrace for a man to be deprived of his. Both sexes often wore a formal high-necked **gown** (or **houppelande**) with trailing sleeves (existing today as the university gown), or a more casual low-necked **cotehardie**. Women and girls wore padded head-rolls (**chaplets**).

1400's

- hat with brooch
- high-necked short gown (houppelande)
- hanging sleeves
- hose
- low-necked cotehardie
- kirtle
- unbelted gown
- chaplet
- fret
- veil
- high-necked gown (houppelande)
- kirtle

Farmworker, 1340

hat
hood
tunic
boots

coif

tunic hitched over girdle

Farmworker, 1300

PEASANTS IN THE MIDDLE AGES, 800-1400

Life was hard. All cloth had to be spun and woven by **hand**, and even **needles** were difficult to get. Clothes made at home with such effort were kept as **loose** and **simple** as possible. Peasants' styles changed little over this period, and indeed

---

PICTURE GLOSSARY, 800–1400

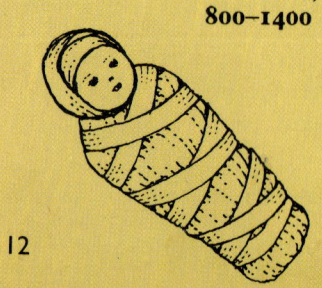

Swaddling was cocooning a baby's body from neck to toe in wide bandages to make its arms and legs grow straight. Practised from before the time of Christ until about 1800 AD.

Underwear. Everybody wore under their tunics a sort of long, full vest with sleeves, called a **chemise**. By 1300 the women's chemise was called a **smock**, and the man's a **shirt**.

at first there was little difference between styles of rich and poor, except in the quality of the material and in the decoration. Peasants wore mostly **wool** and linen. In fact, after 1363, English peasants by law *had* to wear coarse materials, a plain linen girdle and no fur. **Dyes** made from roots and flowers gave only soft hues to peasants' clothes.

Farmworkers

veil
kirtle
sideless surcote
apron
1340

hood
tunic
1320

veil
kirtle hitched over girdle
smock
1410

Pockets. Until 1500's for men and 1800's for women, pockets were not built into clothes, but were usually separate little leather or cloth bags hanging from the waist.

Wimple. A simple form of headdress worn by wealthy and poor women alike. It was a piece of linen draped round the head and pinned under the chin. Still worn by some nuns.

First printed books

Leonardo da Vinci

The gown lost its trailing sleeves, and was worn over a **doublet** (a development of the **gipon** of the 1300's) and **hose**. The casual hood became a respectable turban called a **chaperon**, with the old liripipe used as a scarf. Women's headdresses grew ever bigger and bulkier, but their daughters wore simple **hoods**.

1450's

chaperon

neck-chain

hood

doublet

padded roll

fret

gown

hose

kirtle

long gown (worn over doublet and hose)

gown

Columbus

Age of Exploration

France became the leader of fashion and fine ladies adopted high-waisted gowns with trailing skirts. They wore a variety of charming, but impractical headdresses, above specially shaved foreheads. Younger men sported shorter pleated **jerkins** edged with fur, and their **shoes** grew so long that sometimes they had to be chained to their knees!

1480's

hat
shirt
doublet
short gown
hose
pointed shoes

Turkey bonnet
doublet
gown

jerkin with hanging sleeves

butterfly headdress

The Renaissance

Martin Luther

As trade grew and merchants prospered, clothes became suitably dignified. Men wore squarish hats (still seen in the clergymen's **biretta**), square shoes, and long, fur-trimmed **gowns** over **doublet** and **hose**. Women and girls wore square **gable headdresses** (**English hoods**). They hung purses, keys and **pomanders** from their belts.

1500's

hat
doublet
purse
gown
square-toed shoes

shirt
slashed sleeves
doublet

English hood
gown

English hood
gown
purs
kirtle

Copernicus

Prayer book in English

Clothes became very splendid. Men's clothes got even squarer, with vast padded sleeves cut in places (**slashed**) to show the rich **linings**. Men wore huge padded breeches called **trunk hose** and flat, feathered **bonnets**. Women's skirts were split to show the richly embroidered **underskirt**. The round **French hood** became popular.

1540's

- short gown
- shirt
- slashed sleeves of doublet
- coif
- separate sleeves tied on
- French hood
- stomacher
- padded trunk hose
- doublet
- short gown
- gown over farthingale
- nether stocks
- underskirt

America explored

Elizabeth I

Most people, even the little **unbreeched boy** (see also page 21), wore neck **ruffs**. Men, women and even children wore **stays** or **corsets**. Men and boys wore a sleeveless **jerkin** over their stiffly padded doublets. The bodice (**stomacher**) of women's gowns was also padded. To hold out their wide skirts women wore a **farthingale** (see page 20).

1570's

brimless bonnet
ruff
wings
doublet
trunk hose
garter
nether stocks
wings
underskirt
wings
doublet
jerkin
stomacher
unbreeched boy
Venetians
French hood
gown over Spanish farthingale
neck frill

18

Shakespeare

Gunpowder Plot

Court ladies now had an even larger farthingale under their huge, ankle length skirts. They wore a stiffened fan-shaped **collar** and many long **necklaces**. Decorative strips of material from the shoulder were all that were left of their hanging sleeves. Boys continued to wear longer breeches (as they had in the 1570's) and a downturned collar: a **falling band**.

1600's

- wired collar
- false hanging sleeves
- stomacher
- ankle length gown over French farthingale
- falling band
- breeches
- boots
- spurs
- wired cap
- false hanging sleeves
- rattle
- pomander
- neck chain
- circular cape
- doublet
- trunk hose
- upper stocks (canions)
- stockings rolled-up

19

Farmworkers, 1460

hat with flaps
jerkin
boots

hat
apron
shirt
separate hose

kerchief
gown

THE GROWTH OF THE MIDDLE CLASSES, 1400-1600

The male farmworkers on this page wear simple clothes based on **jerkin** and **hose.** They wear no ruffs. However, the country folk opposite are better off and better dressed. In fact, they represent the merging of the sharp difference between rich and poor of the previous period,

PICTURE GLOSSARY, 1400–1600

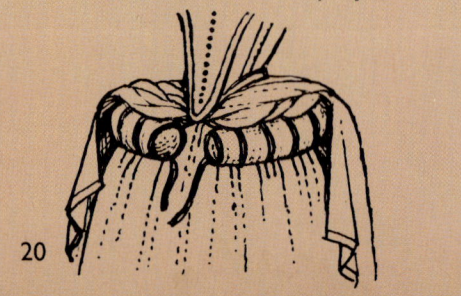

Farthingale. This was to make the skirt stick out. It was either a padded roll worn just below the waist, or an underskirt stiffened with wire or whalebone.

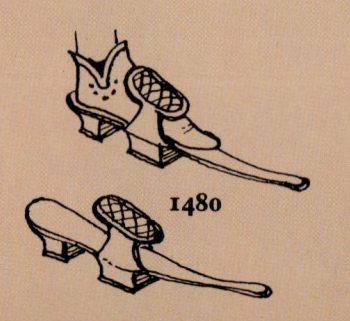

1480

Pattens. In the 1400's were very fashionable, and worn indoors as well as out to keep the feet off the dirt underfoot. Their wooden soles were made longer than the actual shoe.

and the beginning of a so-called **"middle class"**. Hose fit better because of the **knitting machines** invented about 1550. Middle class men's breeches were less puffed out than the fine gentlemen's, but they did wear ruffs. On the whole, middle class women did not wear farthingales and their underskirts, if showing at all, were much plainer.

Countryfolk

jacket

breeches

1587

coif

bonnet

1563

hat

kerchief

muffler

apron

gown

1570

Breeching. Little boys were dressed like little girls in a long frock and cap, until they were 6 or 7, when they were put into breeches. "Breeching" was an occasion for a family party.

Leading strings were decorative strips of material attached to the shoulders of a child's dress and used as controlling reins when the child was learning to walk.

The Pilgrim Fathers

William Harvey

Loops of **ribbon** and masses of **slashing** now ornamented the clothes of both sexes. Men wore high-heeled **boots** with **spurs**, and their breeches now reached the knee. Ruffs were getting lower and the boy's **lace collar** hints at later adult styles. Women left off farthingales so their dresses were less stiff. They no longer showed their underskirts.

1620's

falling ruff
jerkin
doublet
"Vandyke" collar
false hanging sleeve
falling ruff
virago sleeves
slashing
cloak-bag breeches
heeled boots
closed gown (i.e. not showing underskirt)

Milton

English Civil War

Both sexes had magnificent **lace** collars and flowing curls. Men and boys wore broad-brimmed feathered **hats**. These dashing **"Cavalier"** styles contrast with the quieter clothes worn at the same period by the Puritans (see page 24). The two styles typify the two sides in the English Civil War—**Cavaliers** and **Roundheads**.

1640's

- doublet
- slashed sleeves
- "Vandyke" collar
- cloak
- coif
- breeches
- bucket-top boots
- open gown with matching underskirt
- breeches
- closed gown

Far Eastern Trade

Oliver Cromwell

The Puritans wore clothes cut on similar lines to the Cavaliers, but usually in sober **blacks** and **browns**. They mostly cut their hair **short** (hence the name "Roundhead"). They were fond of starched **white linen** collars, cuffs and aprons, and women wore a modest **cap**. Out of doors, both sexes wore **tall hats** like the traditional Welsh hat.

1650's

coif

collar

coif

apron

leading strings

breeches

tall hat without ribbons

breeches

stockings

red-heeled shoes

24

Louis XIV

Great Fire of London

When Charles II regained the British throne, fashions there became as gay as those at the French court. For a few years men wore the ridiculous **petticoat breeches**, and covered their hair with long curly **wigs**. Older boys dressed like their fathers, but the little **unbreeched** boy on **leading strings** (see p. 21) is dressed rather like his sister.

1660's

tall hat with ribbons

falling band

short doublet

cap

low-necked gown

stomacher

leading strings

petticoat breeches

shoe rose

square-toed shoes with red heels

apron

underskirt

25

Scientific discoveries

Peter the Great

A most important change has happened in men's clothes. After nearly 400 years the doublet and hose were finally abandoned. Men and boys wore a tailored collarless **coat**, **knee breeches** and **cravat** (ancestors of today's jacket, trousers and tie). Women and girls wore a tall cap (a **fontange**) and looped back their dresses to show their underskirts.

1690's

Labels on figures:
- wig
- cravat
- ribbons
- collarless coat
- breeches
- stockings
- red-heeled shoes
- hat
- fontange
- leading strings
- long hair
- cravat
- wired fontange
- patch
- gown
- mask
- underskirt

26

Bach

Farming improvements

The white wigs worn by men (like judges' wigs today) were powdered with flour or starch; boys still usually wore their own hair, although some unlucky ones had wigs. Ladies' dresses got fuller, being held out by **hoops** (see p. 30). A long fold of material called a **sacque** hung down from their shoulders. They wore little lace caps and carried **fans**.

1720's

powdered wig

coat

pinner cap

apron

long hair

stockings rolled up

waistcoat

pinner cap

sacque

hooped skirt

Roads improved

Bonnie Prince Charlie

Men's clothes gradually got quieter in colour, as elegant **cut** became more important than fancy trimmings. Sometimes they tucked the ends of their wigs (rather like barristers' wigs today) into a little black bag (a **bag wig**). Women and girls wore their own hair, and fancy **aprons**. Out of doors they perched huge straw hats on top of their lace caps.

1740's

bag wig

coat

buckled shoes

stomacher

apron

wig

collarless coat

mob cap

muslin kerchief

hooped dress

apron

underskirt

28

George Washington

Australia discovered

The tailored coat was so uncomfortable that men tried a looser coat called a **frock.** Their hat brims were turned up to make three-cornered, or **tricorne,** hats. Copying the French queen Marie Antoinette who played at farming, women wore shorter dresses rather like those worn by shepherdesses and milkmaids. They wore high powdered wigs (p.31).

1770's

tricorne hat

frock coat with collar

stock

breeches

jacket

frilly collar

decorated hat

hoops

COUNTRY AND TOWNSFOLK, 1600-1770

Throughout this period, country and the poorer townsfolk still wore a simpler version of the current fashions. **Pattens** were no longer high fashion; they differed from the ones worn in the Middle Ages in being wooden soles raised on round metal rings. In the 1600's,

Labels on figures:
- 1640: cap, gown, pattens
- 1670: own hair, coat
- 1640: hat, cap, kerchief, apron

PICTURE GLOSSARY, 1600-1770

1640

Masks and Patches. Masks protected faces against the sun. Patches made of taffeta were stuck on as an ornament. They were worn by both men and women.

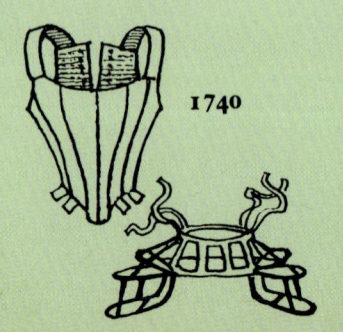

1740

Stays and Hoops. Stays (or corsets) made of whalebone were worn even by children. Hoops of cane, wire or whalebone pushed out skirts.

30

less well off men did not wear the fashionable ribbons. In the 1700's they wore thick woollen or leather breeches, and often **round hats**. Craftsmen's trades were distinguished by their **aprons** (e.g. butchers wore blue). Country labourers wore a simple **smock**. Women wore wool dresses with aprons, and often red **petticoats** underneath.

neckerchief — *hat* — *coat* — *leather apron*
Carpenter, 1755

hat over cap — *gown* — *apron*
Seamstress, 1732

smock
Farmworker, 1750

1770

Wigs and Hair
Women piled their powdered and curled hair into enormous shapes over small cushions and decorated them with fruit, flowers and even ships under full sail. The edifice often stayed that way for weeks.

1770

Calashs. Umbrellas were not popular for a long time, so women protected their elaborate hairdos on wet days with calashes, large folding hoods.

French Revolution

Catherine the Great

New discoveries in farming made this the age of solid prosperity and the country house. Britain, typified by **John Bull**, led men's fashion. Women wore high-waisted hoopless dresses, with fancy **bonnets**. For the first time children had styles of their own. Boys wore loose trousers held up by braces called **gallowses.** Girls wore simple muslin dresses.

1790's

- round hat
- wig
- cutaway coat
- tight breeches
- top boots
- mob cap
- bonnet
- muff
- spencer
- high-waisted dress
- loose pantaloons

Napoleon

Battle of Waterloo

A tax on hair powder in Britain caused it to be abandoned, and the age dawned of elegant dandies like **Beau Brummel**, with padded shoulders and tightly **corseted** waists. **Trousers** became generally fashionable, and women followed the simple styles of Republican Greece and Rome, with straight **muslin dresses** in white or pastel colours.

1810's

gypsy hat

high-waisted muslin dress

parasol

skeleton suit

low top hat

collar

stock

tail coat

trousers

gaiters

low-heeled shoes

33

Transatlantic steamships

Charles Dickens

The Industrial Revolution made the middle class rich, and respectability became the order of the day. Most men wore **frock coats** and tall silk **top hats**. Women's sleeves, hats and skirts ballooned out. Trousers were the basis of all children's fashion—even girls wearing frilly **pantalettes** (see page 40). Young boys wore **tunics**; older boys wore "Eton" jackets.

1830's

tall top hat

frock coat

"pegtop" trousers

hat

cap

pantalettes

peaked cap

"Eton" jacket

tunic

trousers

gigot sleeves

reticule

shorter dress

34

Florence Nightingale

Railway boom

The vast dress skirts were held out by **crinolines** (see page 41). Women wore caps indoors and **bonnets** out, while girls shivered in their flimsy **low-necked** dresses. Babies wore **long clothes** (see page 40). For informal wear, men wore **lounging jackets**. Boys' matching jackets, waistcoats (sometimes called **vests**) and trousers hinted at the adult lounge suit.

1850's

lounging jacket

bow tie

low-necked frock

matching suit

indoor cap

long clothes

crinoline skirt

narrower trousers

pantalettes

decorative underskirt

35

Partition of Africa

Karl Marx

Sewing machines and paper patterns made **tailored** clothes easier to make for all. Women and girls wore **bustles** (see page 41). **Buttoned boots** and **gaiters** were everywhere. The hat called a **bowler** in Britain and a **derby** in America, and the **caped greatcoat** were very popular with men. Boys often wore knee-length **knickerbockers**.

1880's

Bowler, or derby, hat

caped greatcoat

hat

bustle

gaiters and boots

knickerbocker suit

hat

tightly-corseted waist

Sigmund Freud

Early motor cars

Cars and trains made travel generally easier, so clothes for holidays and sport were invented. Men adopted knickerbockers with a **Norfolk jacket** for country wear, and women wore the tailor-made **two-piece costume**, with blouse, achieving a tightly corseted **"hourglass"** figure. For many years children were often dressed in **sailor suits**.

1890's

boater
leg of mutton sleeve
bolero
blouse
tailor-made two-piece costume
skirt
sailor suit
knickerbockers
sailor hat
sailor blouse
long socks
peaked cap
high stiff collar
Norfolk jacket
knickerbockers
gaiters

37

Telephone developed

The Wright Brothers

The last years before World War I glittered with prosperity. Women wore Paris-inspired costumes of great elegance, with lavish **fur, feathers** and **jewelry**. Children's clothes were still rather frilly, but getting looser. Some unlucky boys had to endure the Cavalier-style suit worn by the storybook **Little Lord Fauntleroy**.

1900's

top hat

frock coat

pin-stripe trousers (no crease or turnups)

loose coat over dress

black stockings

boots

Fauntleroy suit

large "picture" hat

corsets underneath to give small waist

fox fur

38

Marie Curie

Russian Revolution

Although men still wore stiff collars, the **lounge suit** was well established and has continued till today with only minor changes. Women's skirts were narrowing. Children's clothes were losing their scratchy, bulky petticoats and becoming more comfortable, with **long socks** and **shoes** gradually replacing buttoned boots and black stockings.

1910's

lounge suit

linen suit

Norfolk jacket (with knickerbockers)

hair bow

sash

crease in trousers

white frock

handbag

socks

spats

turn-ups

shoes

narrower skirt

39

THE WORKING CLASSES, 1770–1910

Trousers and **neckerchiefs** were worn by working men. Working women's skirts were shorter to make cleaning easier. They stuffed them with many **petticoats** instead of crinolines, but they managed some kind of bustle even if made only of newspaper. The **pinafore** was almost a uniform for girls.

Collier, 1814 — hat, waistcoat, jacket, gaiters

Farm girl, 1815 — blouse, skirt

Farmworker, 1815 — neckerchief, hat, jacket, trousers

PICTURE GLOSSARY, 1770–1910

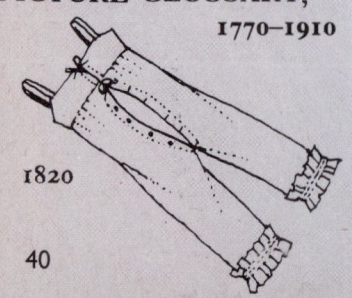

1820

Pantalettes were frilly trousers worn by girls and women under their skirts to hide their legs which in the 1800's were considered indecent. Sometimes these were only separate leg tubes tied on at the knee, called false drawers.

1850

Long clothes. After the end of the custom of swaddling, young babies were put into very long dresses. They were put into shorter dresses when they started to crawl.

However, gradually aids to cheap smart dressing were invented, such as **power looms, sewing machines, paper patterns, waterproofing, elastic, dry cleaning,** and brighter **chemical dyes.** The 1900's added **man-made fibres, zips,** and **permanent waves.** People gradually learned to choose clothes according to age rather than wealth.

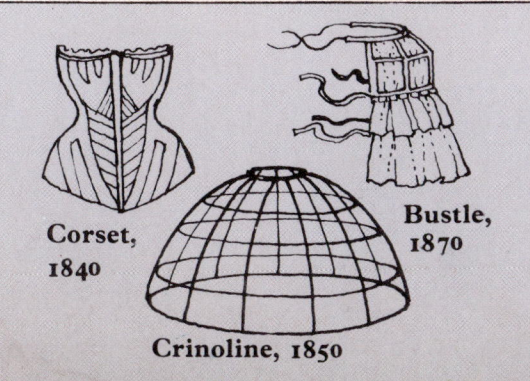

cap
muffler

Crossing sweeper 1860

pinafore
peaked cap
shawl
coat
jacket
trousers tied at knee
dress
buttoned boots
trousers
apron
skirt
boots

Navvy, 1890

1890

1890

Corset, 1840

Crinoline, 1850

Bustle, 1870

Corsets forced the figures into the fashionable tiny handspan waist. The **crinoline** was a steel cage to keep the skirts out. Later the **bustle,** a pad worn at the back below the waistline, was adopted.

1890

Bloomers. About 1850 Mrs Amelia Bloomer wore loose baggy trousers (nicknamed "bloomers"). But women did not really adopt trousers until the 1890's and then only for sport.

41

Atomic discoveries

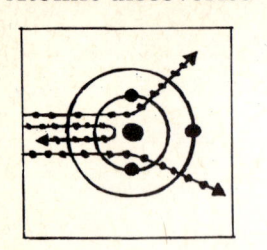

Mahatma Gandhi

Women gained greater freedom after World War I, so they bared their legs to the knees, lowered their waistlines and **shingled** their hair. **Makeup** once again became respectable. Very smart young women were called **flappers**. Boys wore short trousers, assuming long trousers at 13. Often girls wore a comfortable jersey and **skirt**.

1920's

boater

lightweight summer suit

woollen cap

coat

low-brimmed hat

beads

flesh-toned stockings

short-skirted, low-waisted dress

two-tone shoes

leggings

grey flannel suit

high-heeled shoes

42

F. D. Roosevelt

The Great Depression

Women's skirts were longer and so were men's coats. The casual **slouch**, or **Trilby hat** was as typical for men as the **fox fur** for women. **Soft collars** for men were now generally acceptable. The **grey flannel suit** for boys (with short or long trousers) is still with us. The girl's **waisted dress** lasted until the unwaisted shift dress of the 1960's.

1930's

Trilby (or slouch) hat
soft collar
overcoat
wide trousers
grey flannel suit
long socks
cotton frock
sandals
ankle socks
hat worn at angle
fox fur
longer skirt
high-heeled "court" shoes

43

World War II

Winston Churchill

During World War II, styles did not change, although skirts got shorter, because of the lack of material. **Fancy hats**, however, boosted morale. Both sexes wore wide padded shoulders. Boys wore **shirts** and **short trousers**, and girls **blouses** and **skirts**. Little boys wore a **buster suit**, with the trousers buttoned onto the top.

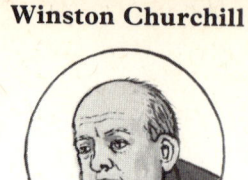

1940's

- double-breasted lounge suit
- blouse
- bolero
- skirt
- buster suit
- pullover
- fancy hat
- padded shoulders
- jacket
- short skirt
- wedge-heeled shoes

John F. Kennedy

First Space Flight

Everyone dressed casually (without hats) for all except very formal occasions, and **trousers** could be worn by women. After the scarcity of the war years, women blossomed into full skirts held out by many **petticoats. Nylon stockings** were generally available. Chain stores and man-made materials made cheap, well-made clothes available to all.

1950's

scarf
sweater
narrower trousers
turn-ups

duffel coat
pony tail
jeans
canvas shoes for play

sweater
casual trousers

hat not necessary
full skirt
ankle-strap shoes

45

GLOSSARY/INDEX

"M" means Male; "F" means Female; "Middle Ages" means the period between 800's and 1400's; in the glossary, but not in the main text, the expression "1500's", "1600's" etc. means the garment was worn over all or most of the whole century. Where the meanings are similar to the clothes worn today, no definition has been given.

Apron (F): *1200's on*, pp. 13, 17, 20, 21, 24, 30, 31. The *1800's* children's version was called a **"Pinafore"**, p. 41. *From early 1600's*, also a fancy covering, pp.19, 24, 25, 27, 28.
    (M): worn by craftsmen and tradespeople, p. 31.
Bag-wig (M): *1700's*, see **"Wig"**.
Band: *1500's and 1600's*, see **"Collar"**.
Bandages (M): *Middle Ages*, strips wound round braies, p. 7.
Barbette (F): *Middle Ages*, white chinband, p. 9.
Bloomers (F): See Picture Glossary, p. 41.
Blouse (F): *1800's on*, pp. 37, 40, 44.
Boater (M and F): *1800's on*, a straw flat hat, pp. 37, 42.
Bolero (F): *1850's on*, short, often sleeveless, jacket, pp. 37, 44.
Bonnet (M and F): *Middle Ages on*, small close-fitting hat, usually without a brim, pp.17, 18, 21. See **"Turkey Bonnet"**.
    (F): *1800's*, headdress with a brim only at the front, tied under the chin, p. 32.
Boots (M and F): *Middle Ages on (and earlier)*, p.10, and through book. Some are **"Bucket-top" (M)**, p. 23; **"Buttoned" (M and F)**, pp. 36–41; **"Top Boots" (M)**, p. 32.
Bowler Hat (M): *1860's on*, hard felt hat invented by hatter William Bowler. Called **"Derby"** in America, p. 36.
Braces (M): *1780's on*, straps to hold up trousers, p. 32. Called **"Suspenders"** in America.
Braies (M): *Middle Ages*, loose trousers, pp.7, 8.
Breeches (M): *1600's on*, trousers stopping at the knee, pp. 19–26, 29–32. Some kinds shown are **"Cloak-bag"**, p.22; **"Petticoat"**, p.25; **"Venetians"**, pp. 5, 18. See also **"Hose"**.
Breeching (Boys): See Picture Glossary, p. 41; pp. 18, 25.
Bustle (F): See Picture Glossary, p. 41; also p. 36.
Butterfly Headdress (F): *Late 1400's*, wired veil, p. 15.
Calash (F): See Picture Glossary, p. 31.
Canions (M): *Late 1500's/early 1600's*, see **"Hose"**.
Cap (M and F): *Middle Ages on*, small close-fitting head covering, pp.19, 24, 25, 30, 31, 34, 35. Worn indoors by women from 1500's to 1800's. Some are **"Mob Cap"**, pp.28, 32; **"Pinner"**, p. 27. See also **"Coif"** and **"Fontange"**.
    (M): *1800's*, peak added, pp. 34, 37, 41.

Cape (M and F): See **"Cloak"**.
Chaperon (M): *1400's*, draped headdress, p. 14.
Chaplet (F): Various meanings but *1300's on*, padded head roll, pp.9–11.
Chemise (M and F): See Picture Glossary, p.12.
Cloak (M and F): *Middle Ages on (and also before)*, loose, wraparound garment, pp.6–9, 23. The shorter kinds were often called **"Capes"**, p. 19. Very long, trailing formal ones were called **"Mantles"**, pp. 7, 8.
Coat (M): At various periods another name for the tunic, the gipon, the doublet, and the jerkin! *1650's on*, the word gets its modern meaning; also the similar garment worn by women and girls, pp. 26–45. See also **"Frock"**.
Coif (M): *Middle Ages*, cap worn under hat or hood, pp. 8, 12.
    (F): *1500's on*, cap, pp.17, 21, 23, 24.
Collar (M and F): p. 11 and throughout book. The *1500's and 1600's* name was **"Band"**. One kind shown is the many-pointed **"Vandyke"**, pp. 22–23. See also **"Ruff"**.
Corsets (M and F): See **"Stays"**.
Cotehardie (M and F): *1300's and 1400's*, see **"Supertunic"**.
Cravat (M): *1600's on*, loose neckcloth tied in knot, p.26
Crinoline (F): See Picture Glossary, p.41; *also* p. 35.
Dagging (M and F): *1300's and 1400's*, fancy cutting of clothes into points, scallops, etc., pp.9, 10.
Derby (M): See **"Bowler"**.
Doublet (M): *1400's to 1670's*, a closely fitting, padded jacket-type garment of various lengths, pp. 14–19, 22, 23, 25. The *1300's* name was **"Gipon"**, pp. 9, 10.
Dress (F): *All periods*, general name for an all-in-one gown or frock.
Duffel Coat (M and F): *1940's on*, an informal short coat, p.45.
English Hood (F): *1500's*, pointed headdress, p.16.
Eton Jacket (Boys): *1800's*, short waist-length jacket, p. 34.
Falling Band/Ruff (M and F): See **"Ruff"**.
Fan (F, and very occasionally M): *1550's on*, feathers or folding panels (often ivory) to cool the face, pp.19, 27.
Farthingale (F): See Picture Glossary, p. 20; *also* pp. 17–19.
Fauntleroy Suit (Boys): *Late 1800's and early 1900's*, velvet and lace suit, rather "Cavalier" in style, p.38.
Fillet (M and F): *1200's on*, circular headband, pp. 8, 9, 10.
Fontange (F): *1690's to 1710's*, tall indoor cap, p. 26.
Fouriaux (F): *1100's*, silk sheaths for hair plaits, p. 8.
Fox Fur (F): *Late 1800's and 1900's*, pp.38, 43.
French Hood (F): *1500's*, curved headdress, pp. 17, 18.
Fret (F): *1200's to 1500's*, criss-cross coif or cap, pp. 9–11, 14.
Frock (Frock Coat) (M): *Middle Ages*, a monk's gown. *1700's*,

46

an informal coat with a collar, p. 29, quite different from: *the 1800's version*, the basic formal, full skirted coat, pp. 34, 38.

(F): *1500's and 1600's*, an informal dress; *1800's*, a back-fastening dress, as opposed to a front-fastening **"Gown"**.

(Children): *1600's on*, word used for children's dresses.

Gable Headdress (F): *See* **"English Hood"**, its other name.

Gaiters (M and occasionally F): *1800's on*, buttoned covering for ankle and lower leg, pp. 33, 36, 37, 40.

Gallowses (M): *See* **"Braces"**, the other name.

Gigot Sleeves (F): *At various times in 1800's*, sleeves very full at shoulder and narrow at wrist, p. 34. The *1890's* version was called a **"Leg-of-Mutton"** sleeve, p. 37.

Gipon (M): *See* **"Doublet"**, its later name.

Girdle (M and F): *Middle Ages on (and before)*, pp. 6–8, 12, 13, 15.

Gown (M): *Middle Ages and on to 1600's*, loose top garment of various lengths, worn mostly on formal occasions, pp. 11, 14, 16, 17. Sometimes called **"Houppelande"**.

(F): *Middle Ages on*, an all-in-one dress, pp. 11 and on; also sometimes called **"Houppelande"**. *In 1800's*, an all-in-one front-fastening dress, so differing from the **"Frock"**.

Greatcoat (M and F): *1700's on*, outdoor overcoat, p. 36.

Hanging Sleeves (M and F): *Middle Ages*, wide long sleeves with slits part-way down to let the arm come out, pp. 8, 9, 11, 14–17. *From 1560's*, became purely decorative (**"False Hanging Sleeves"**), pp. 19, 22. *From 1630's*, worn by children as **"Leading Strings"**, pp. 21, 24, 25, 26.

Hat (M and F): *Middle Ages on*, p. 8 and through book.

Hood (M and F): *Middle Ages on*, loose headcovering, pp. 9, 10, 12. **(F)**: Later, word used for various headdresses, pp. 14, 16–18. *See also* **"English Hood"** and **"French Hood"**.

Hoops (F): *See* Picture Glossary, p. 30; *also pp.* 27–29.

Hose (M): *Early Middle Ages, and after c 1660's*, word for separate "stockings", pp. 6–10, 20, 24, 26, 30. *1300's to 1660's*, "hose" meant stockings joined at the top to form "tights", the upper part sometimes being called **"Breeches"**. In *1500's* top part was puffed out and padded (called **"Trunk Hose"**, with the lower part called **"Nether Stocks"**), pp. 17–19. Between *1570 and 1620* part of the trunk hose was extended down the thigh: **"Upper Stocks"** or **"Canions"**, p. 19.

Houppelande (M and F): *1300's and 1400's, see* **"Gown"**.

Jacket (M): *1400's on*, another name for **"Jerkin"**. *1700's*, short garment with sleeves, worn mostly by country folk, labourers, seamen, etc., pp. 40, 41. *1800's*, worn also by gentlemen, pp. 35–37, 39, 42–44.

(F): *1500's on*, short coat ending at waist, p. 29. *1800's*, worn for sport and as part of tailor-made costume, pp. 36 on.

Jeans (M and F): *1900's on*, originally made of "jean", p. 45.

Jerkin (M): *1400's to 1600's*, short jacket, usually sleeveless, but sometimes with hanging sleeves, worn over the doublet which it was very like in shape, pp. 15, 18, 20–22.

Kerchief (F): *Middle Ages on*, head covering (does not mean a handkerchief), pp. 20, 21. **(M and F)**: *1500's*, a neck scarf ("Neckerchief"), pp. 28, 31, 40. *Late 1600's, 1700's*, covering for neck and bodice, p. 30.

Kirtle (F): *From 1100's*, name for the later kind of "tunic", worn under outer layer (but over chemise or smock), pp. 8–11, 13, 14. By *1500's*, kirtle and gown formed a complete "dress", kirtle being the underskirt, p. 16. *See* **"Underskirt"**.

Knickerbockers (M): *1860's on*, baggy breeches, pp. 36–39.

Leading Strings (Children): *See* **"Hanging Sleeves"**.

Leggings (M and F): *1800's on*, extra leg coverings, p. 42.

Leg-of-Mutton Sleeves (F): *1890's, see* **"Gigot Sleeves"**.

Liripipe (M): *1300's and 1400's*, long tail of hood, p. 10.

Long Clothes (Babies): *1650's on*, long frocks, pp. 35, 40.

Lounge Suit (M): *1860's on*, informal three-piece suit—matching jacket, waistcoat (sometimes called **"Vest"**) and trousers, pp. 39, 42–44. In *1900's*, became normal semi-formal wear, and waistcoat was gradually abandoned.

Lounging Jacket (M): *1840's on*, informal jacket, 35.

Mantle (M and F): *See* **"Cloak"**.

Mask (M and F): *See* Picture Glossary, p. 30; *also* p. 26.

Mob Cap (F): *1700's and 1800's, see* **"Cap"**.

Muff (F, and sometimes M): *1550's on*, p. 32, 36.

Muffler (F): *1500's and 1600's*, square of material worn over nose and mouth to keep out dirt and smells, p. 21.

(M): *1800's on*, small neck scarf, p. 41.

Neck-chain (M): *Middle Ages to 1600's*, necklace, pp. 14, 19.

Neckerchief (M): *See* **"Kerchief"**.

Nether Stocks (M): *1500's and 1600's, see* **"Hose"**.

Norfolk Jacket (M): *1880's on*, belted jacket, pp. 37, 39.

Pantalettes (F): *See* Picture Glossary, p. 40; *also pp.* 34–35.

Pantaloons (M): *1790's to 1850's*, close-fitting "tights", first to the knee and later the ankle. Sometimes loose trousers, p. 32.

Parasol (F): *1800's on*, light fancy sunshade, pp. 33, 37.

Patches (F, and M): *See* Picture Glossary, p. 30; *also* p. 26.

Pattens (M and F): *See* Picture Glossary, pp. 20, 30.

Petticoat (F): *See* **"Underskirt"**.

Petticoat Breeches (M): *1660's*, pleated breeches, p. 25.

Pinafore (Children): *1800's, see* **"Apron"**.

Pocket (M and F): *See* Picture Glossary, p. 13; *also* p. 10.

Points (M): *1400's to 1600's*, laces to tie on hose or sleeves.

Pomander (F): *1500's and 1600's*, gold or jewelled ball hung from belt, filled with scent, pp. 16, 18, 19.

47

Pullover (M): *1900's*, p.44.
Reticule (F): *1800's*, soft handbag closed by a cord, p. 34.
Ruff (M and F): *1560's to 1640's*, stiff collar of starched and gathered frills, pp.18, 19, 21. The **"Falling Ruff"** was gathered but not set stiffly, p. 22. Later, it became the **"Falling Band"**, an ungathered collar, pp. 19, 25.
Sacque (F): *1700's*, gown with a pleat falling from the back of the neck, p.27.
Sailor Suit (Children): *1880's to early 1900's*, boys wore suit with sailor collar and knickerbockers or long trousers, p.37. Girls sometimes wore sailor blouses and hats, p.37.
Sash (F): *1500's on*, pp. 32, 33, 39, 40.
Shawl (F):: *1750's on*, square of material round shoulders, p.41.
Shingling (F): *1920's*, cutting hair very short, p.42.
Shirt (M): *Middle Ages on*, garment worn next to skin until vest introduced in 1840's, pp. 12, 15, 20; *1500's on*, the visible parts were decorated with lace, etc., p. 16, and through book.
Shoes (M and F): *Middle Ages on*, various shapes, with or without heels, throughout book.
Skeleton Suit (Boys): *1790's to 1830's*, suit of trousers buttoned to tight jacket, p. 33.
Skirt (F): Part of dress hanging below waist, throughout book; also, a separate garment as today, p. 37.
Slashing (M and F): *1480's to 1650's*, fancy cutting of clothes to show lining, pp. 16–19, 22–23.
Slouch Hat (M): See **"Trilby Hat"**.
Smock (M): *1700's and 1800's*, workmen's short gown, p. 31.
  (F): *Middle Ages*, basic underwear, pp. 12–13.
Socks (M): *Middle Ages on*, p. 7, etc.
  (F): *End 1800's on*, worn by girls, pp. 39, 42–45.
Spats (M): *1800's and 1900's*, an ankle-length gaiter, p. 39.
Spencer (F): *1790's to 1850's*, short jacket, p.32.
Spurs (M, and women when riding): At various periods, worn on heel for riding and for decoration, pp. 19, 22, 23.
Stays (M and F): *1300's on*, stiffened and boned corsets of various styles. See Picture Glossary, pp. 30, 41.
Stock (M): *1700's and 1800's*, high, stiff neckcloth, pp. 29.33.
Stockings (M): See **"Hose"**.
  (F): As today's, but seldom seen until 1900's, pp. 37–38, 41–45.
Stomacher (M and F): *1500's to 1700's*, separate, padded panel tied to front of gown or doublet, pp.17–19, 25, 28.
Supertunic (M and F): *Middle Ages*, loose outer tunic (but not an outdoor garment like the cloak), of various lengths, pp. 6–8. By *1300's*, there were two developments: the usually sleeveless **"Surcote"** was adapted from the tabard worn over the armour by the Crusaders, pp. 9, 10, 13. The **"Cote-hardie"** was an informal, low-necked garment, of various lengths, with elbow-length hanging sleeves, pp. 9, 11.
Surcote/Surcoat (M and F): See **"Supertunic"**.
Swaddling (Babies): See Picture Glossary, p.12; also p. 7.
Sweater (M and F): *1890's on*, p.45. See also **"Pullover"**.
Tailor-made Costume (F): *1870's on*, matching coat and skirt, made by a tailor, not a dressmaker, pp. 37, 44.
Top Hat/Topper (M): *1800's on*, tall silk hat, pp. 33, 34, 38.
Tricorne Hat (M): *1700's*, three-cornered hat, p. 29.
Trilby Hat (M): *1890's on*, soft felt hat, p. 43.
Trousers (M, and later F): *Late 1700's on*, of varying lengths, with and without creases and turn-ups. Worn by lower classes until *early 1800's*, when they were worn by all men, pp. 33 on. Worn by women generally from 1940's, p. 45.
Trunk Hose (M): See **"Hose"**.
Tunic (M and F): *Middle Ages (and earlier)*, loose garment of varying lengths, pp. 6–13. By *1200's*, men's version sometimes called a **"Cote"** and women's a **"Kirtle"**. In *1800's*, a full knee-length garment worn by young boys, p.34.
Turkey Bonnet (M and F): *1400's and 1500's*, tall brimless hat, p. 15.
Underskirt (F): *1500's on*, name for part of skirt (previously called **"Kirtle"**) shown by opening or looping up gown or dress, pp.17, 18, 23, 25, 26, 28, 29, 35. Sometimes called **"Petticoat"** until *1800's*, when "petticoat" always meant underwear, as today.
Veil (F): *Middle Ages on*, pp. 6–8, 11, 13. Worn by brides from *1800's on*.
Vest (M): *1800's, and in America*, name for **"Waistcoat"**.
  (M and F): *1840's on*, undergarment as today.
Virago Sleeves (F): *1600's*, puffed, padded and slashed sleeves caught in at elbow with ribbons, p. 22.
Waistcoat (M): *1670's on*, an undercoat, often embroidered, pp. 27 on. Its length gradually got shorter, and finally *in 1900's* it became normal not to wear one. Also called **"Vest"**.
Wig (M and F): False hair worn often in *1500's and 1600's*, and all the time by fashionable people in *1700's*, see pp. 25–27, 29, 30, 32. One kind shown is **"Bag wig"**, p. 28.
Wimple (F): See Picture Glossary, p. 13.
Wings (M and F): *1540's to 1640's*, stiffened half circles worn on shoulders, pp. 18, 19, 21, 22.

48